Expanded Second Edition

REBORN IN
CANADA

Personal Privacy
— through —
A New Identity

Trent Sands

Loompanics Unlimited
Port Townsend, Washington

DISCLAIMER

This book in no way condones illegal activity! It is *your* responsibility to determine the legality of your actions. Further, because we have no control over the workmanship, materials, tools, methods, or testing procedures employed, we hereby disclaim any responsibility for consequences resulting from the fabrication or compounding of any item described in this book. We cannot and will not accept any responsibility for this information and its subsequent use. This book is sold for informational purposes only!

REBORN IN CANADA, Expanded Second Edition
© 1991 by Loompanics Unlimited
All Rights Reserved
Printed in USA

Published by:
Loompanics Unlimited
PO Box 1197
Port Townsend, WA 98368

ISBN 1-55950-058-1
Library of Congress
   Catalog Card Number 90-064008

CONTENTS

INTRODUCTION

Canada offers many opportunities for the new identity seeker. The Canadian lifestyle is very close to that of the United States, and Canada's superior social programs, such as universal medical insurance, make Canada all the more attractive. It is possible to create a new identity in Canada, but the Canadian identification system, although similar to the U.S. system, differs in important ways. Once you understand the Canadian system, it is easy to penetrate, and the classic methods of identity changing work very well.

- 1 -

IDENTIFICATION

IN

CANADA

The Canadian identification system consists of two levels. Most of your identification will be issued by a provincial government, which is the equivalent of a state government in the U.S. Federally issued identification in Canada consists of the Canadian passport and the vital social insurance card. Provincially issued identification consists of birth certificates, medical identity cards, drivers licenses and provincial identity cards. Here is where one big difference between the U.S. and Canada arises. In Canada, birth certificates and social insurance cards are considered proper identification in and of themselves. In the United States, a birth certificate is not generally thought of as a piece of identification. It is only used when being issued a piece of identification, such as a drivers license, but not operationally — as identification when cashing a check, for example.

In Canada, the opposite is true. Canadians do use birth certificates and social insurance cards as identity documents to cash checks, for proof of age, etc. The reason for this is in the early 1960's the Canadian federal government encouraged provincial governments to issue plastic-coated wallet-sized birth certificates. Over time the usage of the larger paper birth certificates, which are used in the United States, stopped. The end result is that most Canadians carry a wallet copy of their birth certificate with them. The same happened with the Canadian social insurance card. In the United States, Social Security cards are not considered identification in their own right. The Canadian social insurance card is considered as primary identification. The card is similar to a credit card with number and signature. The card is considered to be primary identification because only citizens or legally admitted permanent residents are entitled to one. Special numbers, easily recognizable, are given to non-permanent residents.

So just about every Canadian carries proof of citizenship with them in their wallet in two forms: proof of birth in Canada and the social insurance card. Canadians born outside of Canada carry a plastic Canadian citizenship card. Contrast this to most Americans, who carry neither birth certificates or social security cards as a matter of routine.

What should be obvious is that a person in Canada who does not carry citizenship proof on his person stands out. Canada has no national identity card, but deliberate policies of the Canadian federal government have seen to it that a de-facto national identity card has been created in the form of wallet birth cards and social insurance cards. A person arrested or detained by police in Canada with only a provincial identity card and drivers license will almost always be asked about their citizenship. In the United States this would be rare unless you are Hispanic or speak with a foreign accent.

The other provincially issued identification is along American lines with the notable exception of the medical identity card. All Canadian provinces provide universal health insurance for a low monthly fee. When a person enrolls into the plan he is issued an identification card that allows free treatment from any doctor in Canada. Hospital care is also covered. Secondary Canadian identification consists of school identity cards, organization cards, library cards, etc. Getting identification in Canada is easy, but special care must be paid to secondary identification early in the process.

Needless to say, as any good identity changer knows, you first must get a mail drop. Get a mail drop that is located inside Canada. This makes the formalities much easier when requesting birth certificates. Some provinces are much tougher about issuing birth certificates. You can find mail drops in any city in Canada by consulting the yellow pages of a Canadian city, or through the book, *Directory of U.S. Mail Drops*, available from Loompanics Unlimited. The procedure is the same as in the U.S., except you will want mail forwarding to your address, or to a postal box in the United States. Everything will be handled through the mail. The first step is the Canadian birth certificate.

- 2 -

CANADIAN
BIRTH
CERTIFICATES

All newly issued Canadian birth certificates are standardized. In the past, each province issued a separate design. Some provinces used lamination, others did not. Now all Canadian wallet birth certificates are issued on green banknote type paper with a border that has lots of engraved type printing on it. The body of the certificate has the provincial seal on it, with the word "Canada" spelled out across it many times. Two examples are shown on the next page.

Another point to realize is that on the back of the certificate is a warning stating the certificate is void if it is laminated. The certificate will also not copy well on an ordinary copier. For these reasons it is recommended that the identity changer use a real birth certificate for his Canadian identity. But as always in the world of identity changing, there are loopholes.

Canadian birth certificates have been standardized.
They are all issued on green banknote paper.

The first is that there are still many of the older issued certificates in circulation. If you know someone with one, you could make a copy of one on a color copier. Some of the older ones copy very well, and when laminated, look 100% authentic. You could place an ad in a Canadian newspaper offering a job, requesting that applicants submit their birth certificate with the application, and saying that it will be returned. Another loophole is that some provinces will still issue a large, paper, certified birth certificate if you can state a legal reason you need it — a court proceeding, for example. These can be copied and altered to create usable new identities.

If you refer to the Canadian birth certificates pictured, you will notice a few things. First, all certificates carry a birth registration number. This number is coded somewhat differently in each province, but allows any birth event to be verified quickly. Some provinces also give each certificate a unique certificate number. The Ontario birth certificate pictured carries this number, whereas the British Columbia certificate does not. This number is very important. This number means each birth certificate issued is unique. If more than one paper tripper starts using this identity, they will run into problems because the computer at the Ontario vital statistics bureau will record all the different certificates being issued under this name. It also means that a birth certificate could potentially be revoked or cancelled, like a drivers license can, sometime in the future.

Much has been said about vital records cross-referencing in Canada. I have obtained many different Canadian birth records of deceased people without any problem. While it is possible that cross-referencing may be attempted in the future, it is not done widely now. Canadian authorities do place the word "Deceased" on birth certificates of very young children, under 3 years of age who die, and on stillborn children. The best protection, as always, is to find a child born in one province who died in another. This is not that difficult because Canadians, like Americans, are very mobile people. Provinces such as British Columbia and Ontario are full of Canadians from other provinces. When, and if, cross-referencing does begin, it will start with records at that future date simply because it is too expensive to go back very far.

The Canadian authorities have also made it easier for the more ambitious identity changer to bypass this entire process. Because all Canadian birth certificates are created on the same paper, all an enterprising person must do is obtain this lithographed paper from a supply house, such as Goes, and find a willing printer to do the background work. Because of the nature of the paper used, Canadian birth documents do not carry embossed or raised seals, as U.S. certificates do. This makes them easier to make once the proper paper is obtained. Standardization is a boon to the identity changer because it means only one form must now be duplicated. The U.S. system, with each state issuing its own style of certificate is more secure because so many different document types would need to be learned, along with embossed seals. This never occurred to the bureaucrats in Canada.

Another avenue is to use the identity of a Canadian citizen born in another country, particularly the United Kingdom. Because so many Canadians were born in Britain, a British birth certificate arouses no curiosity in Canada. Canadians born outside of Canada carry a plastic Canadian citizenship card. If you locate a deceased child who was born in England, you would request his birth certificate from the British authorities. You could then, after having gotten some supporting identification, go to a Canadian citizenship office and ask them to issue you a new Canadian citizenship card. The Canadian death certificate will provide you with all the details of your "parents," and their naturalization information will be on file at the citizenship office. Once you are issued the card, it has the same force as a birth certificate, and can be used when applying for a passport or other identification.

This brings us to actually requesting the birth and death records. I suggest you first write to each provincial vital statistics office requesting the forms you need. What you will receive back will vary widely. Ontario and Alberta have the worst forms, that require enormous amounts of information. Other provinces' forms are relatively simple. In actual practice, you will not use the forms. If you can get from the newspaper accounts of the child's death, the child's birthplace and birthdate, father's name, mother's maiden name and the child's address, you have enough information for the vital statics people to locate the birth record. If you send your request in letter form with this information, along with the correct fee (found from the application form), almost all provinces will send you the certificate without any hassle, to an address within Canada. If you can get the necessary information to do this, always request *both* the wallet sized and larger sized certificates. The reason for this is the larger certificate will have the names and birthplaces of the parents on them. This data you will need later on for the passport application.

If the newspaper account of the child's death does not provide enough information, you will have to request the child's death record first. You will write in the name of the late child's mother or father. Your reason in your letter will be you need it for legal reasons to complete your records. The death certificate will give you the additional information you need for the birth document. One thing which will be obvious from the vital statistics forms in Canada is the provincial governments have a different attitude about people requesting official documents relating to them. You will always be asked to provide a specific reason why you are requesting the document. Always say for a passport or drivers license. You will pay the fee with a money order, with your return address as the mail drop in Canada which you rented before. The addresses of all Canadian vital statistics bureaus are provided at the end of this chapter. Should you go the route of a child born in Great Britain, you can get the appropriate address and forms from any British Consulate in Canada.

CANADIAN VITAL
STATISTICS OFFICES

ALBERTA:

Vital Statistics
10405 100 Avenue
Edmonton, Alberta, T5J-0A6

BRITISH COLUMBIA:

Division of Vital Statistics
1515 Blanshard
Victoria, British Columbia, V8W-3C8

MANITOBA:

Vital Statistics
Norquay Building
Kennedy and York Streets
Winnipeg, Manitoba, R3C-0V8

NEW BRUNSWICK:

Vital Statistics
Box 600
Fredricton, New Brunswick, E3B-5H1

NEWFOUNDLAND:

Division of Vital Statistics
P.O. Box 4750
St. John's, Newfoundland, A1C-5T7

NORTHWEST TERRITORIES:
Vital Statistics
P.O. Box 1320
Yellowknife, N.W.T, X0E-1H0

NOVA SCOTIA:
Vital Statistics/Department of Health
Provincial Building
Halifax, Nova Scotia, B3J-2M9

ONTARIO:
Office of the Registrar General
McDonald Block, Parliament Buildings
Toronto, Ontario, M7A-1Y5

PRINCE EDWARD ISLAND:
Vital Statistics
P.O. Box 3000
Charlotte Town, P.E.I, C1A-7P1

QUEBEC:
Registrar General/Population Registrar
Department of Social Services
845 Joffre Avenue
Quebec City, Quebec, G1S-3L8

SASKATCHEWAN:
Division of Vital Statistics
3475 Albert Street
Regina, Saskatchewan, S4S-6X6

YUKON:

Registrar General
Box 2703
Whitehorse, Yukon, Y1A-T6C

- 3 -

SECONDARY

IDENTIFICATION

Once you have obtained the birth certificate, you will need to get some supporting identification before you can get a provincial identity card, drivers license, or social insurance card. The first one to get is a medical insurance card. All provinces issue them as part of the national health insurance system in Canada. In the province where your mail drop is located, write to the provincial health insurance plan office requesting an enrollment form. You can get the correct address or phone number from the phone directory or from information. The form you will receive is a little different province to province, but is pretty simple. A sample (reduced in size) is shown on page 19.

Because universal medical care is a right in Canada, very little verification takes place. Some provinces may request a copy of your birth certificate, but that is all. On the form you will say that you have never had any previous coverage. If the form does ask for a social insurance number, you can make one up. This is only requested in case later on you want premium payment assistance, and they need to check your tax return. Send in the form with the proper fee, and in a few weeks your medical identity card will be on its way to you.

Another excellent piece of supporting identification is issued by the Canadian Hostelling association. Their membership card has a photograph on it, along with holder's address, birthdate and signature. It is an excellent looking piece of identification, and you can apply for it through the mail. Just consult the telephone book for their address and request an application. I also recommend you get a library card, and a fishing license, which are also easily obtained. Some Canadian cities issue transit passes with a photograph, signature and address on them. These are excellent as well. Some colleges will allow you to register for one course as an extension student, or even offer courses through the mail. You can usually get a student identity card. Once you have this supporting identification, you are ready for the motor vehicle branch people.

Ministry Ontario of Health Health Insurance Plan Ontario	P.O. Box 38 Kingston, Ontario K7L 5J2	For OHIP Use Only

Application for Non-Group Enrolment

Sections 1, 2, 3 and 7 must be completed.

Confidential when completed.

Please see instructions on opposite page

For OHIP Use Only

OHIP Number	Trans code	Type	Stat	Eff. date	To date	TA Reason	ASE	TRN	Station

❶

Surname (family name) *please print*		Initials

☐ Miss ☐ Mr ☐ Mrs ☐ Ms

Mailing Address

If Rural Route or General Delivery, print name by which you are known, i.e. Tom, Mary, etc.

Telephone Number	Date of Birth day month year

Marital status

☐ married ☐ single ☐ divorced

Postal Code

☐ separated ☐ widowed ☐ other

Previous OHIP no., if any	Present employer	Business telephone no.

Please do not remit premiums with this application unless requested to do so. You will be billed as required after your application has been processed.

❷ **Insurable status** ☐ **Single premium** I have no eligible dependent(s) ☐ **Family premium** I have eligible dependent(s)

(Dependents are not covered if not residing in Ontario, except as indicated in part 2 on the reverse side of the application)

Residency status: Complete A, B, C, D or E of this section. Note: Tourists, Transients and Visitors to Ontario are not Eligible to Enrol in OHIP For Your Own Protection Send Photocopies of Immigration Forms, Birth Certificates, or Citizenship Certificates — Not Originals.

❸
A ☐ ☐ Landed Immigrant [Attach photocopy of Canadian Immigration Record or Return-]
☐ Returning Immigrant [ing Resident Permit]
☐ Landed Immigrant from another Canadian Province or Territory

Date of arrival in Ontario Month Year	Previous place of residence	Intended length of stay in Ont.

B ☐ Returning Canadian [Attach photocopy of Canadian birth certificate or Canadian citizenship certificate]

Date of arrival in Ontario Month Year	Previous place of residence	Intended length of stay in Ont.

C ☐ From another Canadian province or territory [Attach photocopy of Canadian birth certificate or Canadian citizenship certificate]

Date of arrival in Ontario Month Year	Name of Canadian Prov. or Territory & expiry date of previous coverage	Intended length of stay in Ont.

D ☐ Ontario resident [Attach photocopy of Canadian birth certificate or Canadian citizenship certificate]

Date of arrival in Ontario Month Year	HOW LONG HAVE YOU LIVED IN ONTARIO?	Years	Months

E If not A, B, C or D (above) please provide applicable information below

☐ Employment Authorization (attach photocopy)   ☐ Minister's Permit (attach photocopy)

☐ Student Authorization (attach photocopy)   ☐ Other provide details on the reverse side of application

Date of arrival in Ontario Month Year	Previous place of residence	Intended length of stay in Ont.

❹ **Applicant changing from dependent-child status**

☐ I became 21 years of age in ____ Month Year } Complete A

A Parents OHIP no

☐ I am under 21 but no longer dependent and request my own coverage ____ } Complete A

B Date of marriage Birthdate of spouse Month Year Month Year

☐ I am under 21 and am now married ____ } Complete A, B & C

C Spouse's OHIP no

☐ My spouse is also under 21 ____ } Complete D

D Spouse's Parent's OHIP no

❺ **Applicant Age 65 or Older** If you qualify as per instructions, check here so we may send you an Application for Premium Exemption ☐

❻ **Premium Assistance** If you qualify as per instruction, check here so we may send you an Application for Premium Assistance ☐

For OHIP Use Only	
Clerk	
Date	

❼ I agree to allow the Ontario Health Insurance Plan to verify all the information I have given in this application.

Signature of applicant	Date

There is a penalty for knowingly filing false information in this application.

105 B2E (B7 12)

Cat No 7510 40R2

An enrollment form for Canada's provincial
health insurance program. A medical insurance card
is an essential piece of supporting I.D.

- 4 -

DRIVERS LICENSES

AND

PROVINCIAL I.D. CARDS

Armed with your birth certificate and supporting identification, you are ready to get a provincial identification card
and drivers license. The provincial identity card should come
first. Most provinces issue the provincial identity card through
the motor vehicle division, but a few issue them through the
provincial liquor control agency. Even better for the identity
changer are those provinces that issue provincial identity cards
through the mail via the liquor board.

The procedure is simple, if you have prepared in advance.
In Canada you will be asked for one piece of primary
identification and one secondary piece. The primary piece is
your birth certificate. The secondary piece can be any
identification with your signature on it. The biggest challenge
is to review the various facts of your new identity. Write it

all out on a sheet of paper: birthdate, birthplace, parents' birthdates, mother's maiden name, etc. When you go for the provincial identity card, the clerk will take your identification, ask you a few questions as to address and other personal data, and take your photograph. In most provinces, your card is mailed to you a few weeks later.

Once you have the provincial identity card, getting the drivers license is a snap. Take a copy of the driver's booklet when you go for the provincial identity card. If you are older and getting a drivers license, it is easier in Canada than in the U.S. because many Canadians do not get drivers licenses until later in life. This is due to the better public transit systems in Canada. However, the clerk will ask you point blank if you have ever had a drivers license before. So be ready to answer "no" convincingly. The test is simple, and after it is over you will be issued a learner's permit, which itself is excellent primary identification. In most provinces you must wait a month before you can take the road test. The best way is to contact a driving school and rent a car for one lesson and the road test. You take the road test, and then are issued a temporary drivers license in most provinces. A few weeks later, the plastic one with photograph will arrive. Some provinces issue a two-part license with a license card and photo card, and some provinces issue permanent licenses on the spot.

Once you have the provincial identity card and drivers license, you are ready to get the most important piece of identification: the Canadian social insurance card. Without this card, you cannot work or survive very long in Canada. But you should not attempt to get it until you have gotten all of the previously mentioned identification. If you would like to see what various Canadian drivers licenses look like, I recommend you order a copy of the current edition of *I.D. Checking Guide* from Drivers License Guide Company, 1492 Oddstad Drive, Redwood City, CA 94063. As license designs can change from year to year, it is pointless to illustrate them here.

- 5 -

SOCIAL INSURANCE CARDS

The social insurance card is the vital piece of identification if you intend to live and work in Canada under your new identity. Unlike the U.S. Social Security number, social insurance numbers are widely used to determine entitlement to a wide array of benefits and privileges. The first difference is that Canadian citizens are only legally allowed to have one social insurance number, and they have almost no right to have it changed. In the United States, millions of people have two or more numbers and an American can get his number changed.

The Canadian social insurance number is a nine digit number broken into 3 groups. The first digit tells what part of the country the number was issued in. The next 7 digits are random, and the last digit of the number is a check digit. If a person is not a resident immigrant or a Canadian citizen, their social insurance number will begin with a nine. You must get a real social insurance number. The reason is that the Canadian number works so much faster than the American one. If you are working under a false social insurance number, the computers at social insurance headquarters in New Brunswick will very quickly spit it out. This will almost immediately start an inquiry to have your employer verify your citizenship status. Most illegal immigrants to Canada are caught this way.

Getting a real social insurance number is not that hard, if you have prepared for it. There are two ways to get the number, in person or by mail. Most people have to apply in person because the only way you can apply by mail is if you live in a small town without an office of the Canadian Employment Commission. One possible way around this would be to rent a postal box in a small town. In towns where people must apply by mail, the post office will have an "application by mail for social insurance number kit." You will have to submit your birth certificate and one other piece of identification. This is sent to New Brunswick and your card will be sent to you in about 3 weeks time. The advantage is obvious, you can avoid the interview with the bureaucrat, but it is not an option for most identity changers.

To prepare to go in person you must become Canadian. Here is where it will be important. Read up on Canada during the time you are getting your other identification and be sure you know your "hometown" well. Most Canadian libraries carry newspapers from all over Canada. Next practice getting a Canadian accent, and learning Canadian terms. This is best done by listening to Canadians speak and also through listening to Canadian radio and television broadcasts. Your cover story will be that you went to a university in the United

States and have now decided to return to Canada. This is an excellent story because thousands of Canadians do this all the time. Another factor working in your favor is that Canada has a high percentage of people who were born in other countries. So older people are commonly getting social insurance numbers for the first time. The procedure will be over in about 10 minutes at the most. The clerk will have you fill out a form, look at your birth certificate and other identification, and send you on your way.

Now you are ready to work in Canada, along with getting your Canadian passport.

- 6 -

CANADIAN PASSPORTS

The first complement to your new Canadian identity is a Canadian passport. Once again it is easy to obtain if you follow careful procedures, but if you are careless, it could lead to the destruction of your entire identity. Some other books that purport to give good information on this subject are filled with fatal errors.

You can obtain a Canadian passport application from any post office within Canada. The application form (reduced in size) is shown on the next two pages. It is quite simple, and if you apply by mail, you must submit your birth certificate. The sticky point is that someone must act as your guarantor who is a Canadian citizen and a member of the listed pro-

A Canadian passport application form.

6. CITIZENSHIP – This information is required to establish your Canadian citizenship. Canadian passports are issued only to Canadian citizens. If you have submitted a certificate of Canadian citizenship issued in or since 1977, it is not necessary to complete (b) and (c).

(a) DOCUMENTARY EVIDENCE OF CANADIAN CITIZENSHIP – Each time you apply for a passport you must provide ORIGINAL DOCUMENTS (not photocopies) which prove you are a citizen of Canada. The documents will be returned. You may be requested to provide additional information or documents to confirm citizenship has been returned.

Title of Document (eg. certificate of birth, record of birth in Quebec, certificate of Canadian citizenship) | Certificate or Registration Number (if applicable) | Date of Issue

(b) ARE YOU NOW OR HAVE YOU EVER BEEN A CITIZEN OF A COUNTRY OTHER THAN CANADA?

Write yes or no — IF YES, indicate by birth / by naturalization | Country | Effective Date

(c) DID YOU RESIDE OUTSIDE CANADA BEFORE FEBRUARY 15, 1977?

Write yes or no — IF YES, give dates for extended periods (more than 3 months). If naturalized in Canada, indicate only those extended periods after naturalization | From | To | From | To

7. MARRIAGE DATA – To be completed if you are or have been married. If the space below is inadequate, attach a separate sheet giving this information for all marriages. Details of marriage(s) are required in connection with identity, citizenship and/or custody of children.

	Date of Marriage Year Month Day	Spouse's Name in full	Spouse's Date of Birth Year Month Day	Spouse's Country of Birth	Spouse's Citizenship Before marriage	At present
Present or most recent marriage						
Previous marriage(s)						

8. PERSON TO NOTIFY IN CASE OF EMERGENCY – It is in your own interest to provide this information.

Name | Relationship

Address (No. Street City Province Postal Code Area Code) | Telephone

WARNING TO ALL APPLICANTS AND GUARANTORS – Section 58(2) of the Criminal Code reads "Every one who, while in or out of Canada, for the purposes of procuring a passport for himself or any other person, makes a written or oral statement that he knows is false or misleading is guilty of an indictable offence and is liable to imprisonment for two years."

9. DECLARATION OF APPLICANT

I solemnly declare that;
(i) the statements made in this application are true,
(ii) the photographs enclosed are a true likeness of me,
(iii) I am a Canadian citizen, and
(iv) I have known my guarantor personally for at least two years (or completed form PPT 132 – "Declaration in Lieu of Guarantor")

Dated (Year Month Day) at (City Province)

Signature (Signature of Applicant)

10. DECLARATION OF GUARANTOR – No fee is chargeable for this declaration. Before this declaration is signed, items 1-9 must be completed.

I, the guarantor, a Canadian citizen residing in Canada,
First Name
Surname (Name of Guarantor)

Guarantor's occupation according to instr. 10
Business address in full (include name of firm or organization)

declare that to the best of my knowledge and belief all the statements made in this application are true. I make this declaration from my knowledge of the applicant whose name is

First Name
Surname (Name of Applicant)

(No. Street City Province Postal Code)
Telephone (Area Code Home / Area Code Business Extension)

whom I have known personally for ____ and whose (State Number) photograph I have certified on the reverse side.

Dated (Year Month Day) at (City Province)

Signature (Signature of Guarantor)

PPT 044 (86-11)

fessional classifications. If you do not have a suitable guarantor, you must complete a supplemental form called "Declaration in Lieu of Guarantor." This form will be checked out and verified by the investigations branch of the passport office, especially if all your documents are newly issued. I suggest you meet a suitable guarantor, rather then run the risk of a passport investigation. Start seeing a local doctor now that you have a medical card, or start attending a small local church. The second is even better because it will allow you to meet other people who can possibly help you later in terms of references, jobs, etc. Even though the form says the guarantor should have known you for 2 years, in actual practice your new Minister or Doctor will probably be willing to give you a reference after a year. Never, ever, forge a guarantor, or create a phoney one. Guarantors are contacted, and their names checked against professional society membership lists.

The other route is to apply for a Canadian passport outside of Canada in the United States. In one way it is easier, because it is accepted that you may not know anyone who can act as your guarantor in the United States. But it is also more difficult to apply from within the United States because you must submit a photocopy of your U.S. Visa. Unlike one book on the subject which says they will give you one at the border, the reality is different.

For a Canadian to have a Visa in the United States means the Canadian either is working in the U.S. on a temporary work permit, or is a resident alien, or some other status that requires a Visa. However, there is a solution. Under recently enacted trade legislation between the U.S. and Canada, Canadians with certain skills will be issued a work permit automatically at the border if they can produce evidence of a job offer. You could, using classic paper trip methods, set up an employer front in Canada using a secretarial service, and create a bogus transcript from a Canadian university. You could apply for jobs in a U.S. city, and once you have the job offer, go to the border. The U.S. Immigration Service will then issue you a work permit. Then you could apply for the Canadian passport from the U.S. For more information on which professions qualify under the new legislation, you should consult the booklet *Treaty Canada* from the U.S. Immigration Service.

My own feeling is the best way to the passport is to meet a suitable guarantor. This way you harden your new identity and at the same time build up a group of acquaintances who can smooth your transition into Canadian society.

- 7 -

EMPLOYMENT, BANKING AND CREDIT

The same techniques that work in the United States for setting up employment references and banking and credit facilities are almost identical in Canada. There are a few differences. The biggest hurdle is employment. You will need to create a local employment reference for yourself so that you can get a job. This is easily done through a secretarial service that will allow you to create a company name, address, and telephone answering service on their facilities. You need only look in the phone book to find them. The explicit details are the same as for the United States, and I urge the reader to consult my other book *Reborn In The U.S.A., Expanded Second Edition,* published by Loompanics Unlimited or the book *How to Steal a Job,* published by Morrison Peterson Publishing, P.O. Box 25130, Honolulu,

Hawaii 96825, for additional details. The problem in Canada comes up if you are a professional person who is seeking more than entry level unskilled or semi-skilled work.

If you have a degree in some field from a U.S. university, you could duplicate your transcripts, putting in your new name and identity particulars on the form. Many thousands of Canadians have American degrees, and this will not raise a lot of questions, especially if you can couple this with a local employment reference that you will create through the secretarial service. The other option is to get a degree from a diploma mill in the United States. This way, should your prospective employer want to check your academic transcripts directly, he can. However, some cautions should be followed with both methods.

If you do go through the diploma mill route, make sure you use one that has an address and telephone number, and that they are willing to verify student records. I suggest that instead of a diploma mill that you use a "university" that is one step higher. These unaccredited universities meet the bare minimum requirements to operate legally, and they will be around to verify student records. You will have to go through a few formalities to get your degree, but in a few weeks you will have it. This will work fine for the interim. I always recommend that the new identity seeker get genuine academic degrees in his new name as soon as possible.

One way to do this would be to apply to a Canadian university in your new city as a 3rd or 4th year transfer student from the U.S. You would submit your altered actual transcript from a real university, but with the last year or two missing. If your grades are good, which you will make sure they are, you will be accepted into the last year or two of your program. You could go part time, and still be able to work, or go full time. As a Canadian student you will pay very low tuition fees, and be eligible for a whole range of grants and loans to finance your schooling. Another route is to use your bogus transcript to get into a graduate program in your field at a Canadian university. This way you can earn a Canadian higher degree. Canadian graduate students get excellent graduate stipends, and it can be a very pleasant year or two to become acclimated to your new identity in a university setting. The third option is to work on a degree through correspondence study. Many Canadian universities offer degree programs through correspondence study, and many U.S. universities will allow Canadian students to use their correspondence courses. You could obtain a real degree this way. I suggest you consult the book *Bear's Guide to Earning Non-Traditional College Degrees* published by Ten Speed Press, P.O. Box 7123, Berkeley, California 94707. But I should say again, mail order degrees and altered transcripts are only an *interim* measure for the new identity seeker. To rely upon them forever creates an Achilles heel in your new Canadian identity.

Banking and credit are simple in Canada. After you have gotten all your Canadian identification and set up your employer front, go to any Canadian bank or credit union and open up a checking and savings account. I prefer Canadian credit unions because the fees are lower and the service is better. The formalities will be over quickly, and in 2 weeks or so you will receive your card for the automated teller machine, which itself is a nice extra piece of identification.

Credit is the other necessary part. To start your Canadian credit rating I suggest you apply for a couple of oil company credit cards. They are the easiest cards to get. You would put your secretarial service company front on the application as your employer. Your home address and telephone are your mail service. You can set your salary, years employed, etc., all to work to your best advantage. More details on this are given in the book *Credit: The Cutting Edge* by Scott French, available from Loompanics Unlimited.

Essentially, these first applications will get your file started at the credit bureau. Use and pay on time these first cards for a few months, and then apply for a bank credit card at your bank or credit union. Within a year's time you will be able to get a loan for whatever purpose you want.

Renting an apartment and arranging telephone service are as easy, if not easier than in the United States. I suggest you create the company front first at the secretarial service before you rent an apartment because some landlords will want an employer reference. Also, it is very easy to rent apartments in an area where university students live. Check this out by visiting the housing office on any Canadian college campus. Telephone service takes all of five minutes to start. The actual application form is huge, but it takes little time. Go in person to start service.

- 8 -

THE

TOTAL CANADIAN

This section is for the person who wants to live in Canada permanently, but under your own name (your original American name). You must take all of the previous steps with regards to your basic reborn identification — drivers license, provincial identity card, etc. If you have not been in any trouble with the Canadian authorities, there is no reason you cannot live in Canada under your true name. Another advantage is that you can then use your former academic records, etc., to help you get established in Canada.

The first step is to find out the procedure for changing your name in the province you wish to live. At most Canadian bookstores you will find do-it-yourself law books that will include something like *Changing Your Name in Ontario,* for example. It usually involves filing a change of name application with the local court, paying to have three days of notices run in a local newspaper or legal gazette, and paying a fee. The whole process will take two to three months.

Once you have the change of name order from the court, you can then send it to "your" province of birth, and the birth certificate will be amended to show your actual name. The only thing that will vary between the old and new you is your birthdate. The nice thing is that the "Canadian" you and the "American" you are totally different in the computer. The different birthdates ensure that. For example, if the "Canadian" you was stopped and given a speeding ticket in the U.S., you would be a totally different person to the computer. No one will link the two of "you." But there are some cautions here.

First, change your name in a different province from the one in which the birth certificate was issued. You never know how many old relatives of the deceased child may still be in the area. Do a little research. Newspaper accounts and notices will usually say how many brothers or sisters the child had, and who his parents were. Look in the telephone book in your new city to make sure they are not there. The court will give you a choice of publishing the name change in either a local paper or the provincial legal gazette. Always pick the legal gazette. Very few people in the general public read it, and you reduce to near zero the chances that a relative would see it. It is all right to utilize your past educational records once you have done this, *but nothing else.* Anything further increases the chances that someone will be surprised to find out that you are "Canadian," or that the differences in birthdates will become known.

Once you have gotten the name change order you can get all your identification changed. You can do this in two ways. The first way is just to go into the Motor Vehicle Branch, and elsewhere. Show them the order, and have them issue new documentation. The second way is even better because it leaves an even fainter trail. Once you have gotten the name change order, send it to the province of birth with your request for a new birth certificate. The new certificate will have a new number on it and the new name. You could then get the supporting identification in your true name. Then you could go the Motor Vehicle Branch, etc. and get all new identification with *no* reference to the name change. You could then get a new social insurance card as well. You could then open a new bank account, and establish credit under your true name. If you go this route, *do not* get any credit cards or loans *before* your name change. Credit bureaus do enter all name changes into their files to check for any matches on current customers. By waiting until after you have changed your name to apply for credit, no link will exist in the credit bureau between you and the old name.

You, of course, would use a different address when you apply for your new identification. The beauty of this method is that the only places that have any record of a name change will be the courthouse where it was done, the legal gazette, and the vital statistics bureau. Over time, these records begin to recede, and unless someone had a reason to think you had changed the name, it would not occur to anyone. Even if they did, you have nothing to worry about anyway. You can even get a passport, because although the application does ask for your surname at birth, it is not checked out unless they have a reason to. Just leave the space blank. As long as your birth certificate is in order, and your guarantor check is positive, you will be issued the passport.

- 9 -

CSIS,

CANADA'S

SECRET POLICE

In the 1970's, the Canadian federal police force, the Mounties, had responsibility for counter-espionage work within Canada. Many abuses occurred and it was decided that the RCMP should be relieved of its duties in this area. The litany of illegal wiretaps, opening of mail, and other actions taken against Canadian citizens was enormous, and far surpassed anything the FBI had done in the U.S.A. In place of the RCMP, the national security service would be a civilian-run agency whose members were not law enforcement officers. In reality, most of the members of the old RCMP security service just joined CSIS. CSIS was given massive powers. CSIS could start investigations of any group or individual if they felt this person or group threatened "National Security" or if, in the case of an organization, they felt it had any type of foreign connections or it was foreign influenced or financed. Essentially, this allows CSIS to start files on anyone at any time.

But this was not the worst part of the legislation creating CSIS. CSIS agents can at any time open any person's mail, tap anyone's telephone, start surveillance of anyone, and is not required to go before a judge to get warrants for any of this. CSIS agents must only have the Attorney General of Canada authorize their request. CSIS agents can also get search warrants in the same manner.

There is no external oversight of CSIS. Unlike the FBI and the CIA, which are subject to overview by many different Congressional Committees, no such real reveiw of CSIS exists. A small review panel consisting of the head of CSIS, the Attorney General and the Prime Minister is the only oversight. CSIS has not used its powers with much discretion either. CSIS has files on nearly 50,000 Canadians and many thousands of organizations. The vast majority of these people and groups are engaged in lawful political dissent. This would be the equivalent of the FBI maintaining active files on one in every 50 Americans.

Unlike the FBI in this country, CSIS is not subject to any meaningful challenges of its files under Privacy Act regulations or Freedom of Information Act regulations. In the United States, an individual can demand, under the Freedom of Information Act, to see files the FBI, or any other government agency, has compiled on him. If the agency does not respond, the plaintiff has the right to sue for release of the information in the U.S. District Court. In Canada, under the Canadian Privacy Act, no such rights exist with regard to CSIS files. The most that can be achieved is for the Privacy Commissioner to examine the files himself. We will have more about this later.

Perhaps the most privacy destroying aspect of CSIS is its reaching of "agreements in principle" with many Canadian Provincial Governments. These agreements in principle allow CSIS officers access to data on individuals held by the province. As pointed out previously, the amount of data is massive. Driver records, health records, tax data, etc. are all held by the province. Most provinces allow CSIS to troll through these databanks at will.

- 10 -

THE CANADIAN DRIVER MASTERFILE

The Canadian Federal Government, in cooperation with the Canadian Provinces, has begun to keep a masterfile of all drivers licenses and vehicle registrations in the country. All provinces agree to send records of all new drivers licenses and vehicle registrations to the Federal Department of Transportation on a regular basis. The Federal Transportation Department then reduces the information into a common code and creates a centralized database with this information. Eventually this database will be added to the database of the Canadian Police Information Computer in Ottawa. When this occurs, Canada will have in essence created a situation where most people's addresses are available to the police, and where this data is constantly updated. This is similar to Germany where people must register their new address with the police when they move. Obviously there would be an out-cry if the Canadian goverment *openly* tried to create such a system. So instead they are doing it quietly.

This new database goes far beyond anything that the provinces have done individually. Now, if a person does not renew a drivers license or does not renew a vehicle regis-tration, after a certain period of time, the computer purges itself of the data. This is a fundamental aspect of privacy in the computer age. After a time, data no longer relevant is destroyed. The new Federal Driver Index will not do this. All data will be retained forever. For example, if a person got his first license in Ontario and registered his first car there, and later moved to British Columbia, ten years later the Federal Driver Index would still show his old Ontario license and vehicle registration. So the Federal Driver Index could, and will, track a person throughout his lifetime.

Another dangerous development is that now provincial governments are starting to design identification documents to meet the needs of private organizations. The Province of Manitoba has redesigned its drivers licenses into a credit card format with a magnetic stripe down the back. This was done to allow merchants to swipe the card through a magnetic card reader to capture the information and place it directly into their database. It is only a matter of time before check cashing services like Telecheck are allowed direct on-line access to Motor Vehicle Records when all drivers licenses are made this way. When that happens, the whole concept of data privacy and "one use" for data would be gone by the wayside.

- 11 -

THE

CANADIAN

PRIVACY ACT

The Canadian Privacy Act is a good example of a typically Canadian approach to civil liberties. On the surface the Canadian Privacy Act seems to be a tiger. It creates the Offices of the Privacy Commissioner. It requires the Federal Government to publish a history of all Federal Government databanks. It requires that the Federal Government release data that it holds on an individual within a 60 day period. If this information is not released, the Privacy Commissioner will then intervene to get the information. It sounds good, but then come all of the exemptions.

Exemptions exist in the form of "closed" databanks. When an agency like CSIS is allowed to maintain all of its records in a closed database, it means a privacy act request will be denied. At that point all the privacy commissioner can do is to review the data himself. He cannot confirm or deny the existence of the record, and will only issue a cryptic statement to the effect that the "complainant's concerns have been investigated." That is all. Of course, all of the files that people really want to see are in "closed" databases. These include CSIS, the RCMP, the Solicitor General's Department, etc.

The Canadian Privacy Act does allow for some court review of denial of access, but the Court review is very limited. The Court review only applies to the denial of the information, not to the actual *collection of the data,* or to *errors contained in the data.* The best explanation of the Canadian Privacy Act comes from the Privacy Commissioner himself. Appendix Four contains excerpts from the Privacy Commissioner's 1986 Annual Report.

- 12 -

CONCLUSION

For the new identity seeker, the only way to keep your privacy in Canada is to use the classic methods of "paper tripping" in Canada. Your privacy will depend on the fact that you have previously decided that the computers will contain only the data you want them to provide.

- 13 -

RECOMMENDED

READING

NEW I.D. IN AMERICA
by Anonymous
Paladin Press
PO Box 1307
Boulder, CO 80306

THE PAPER TRIP I & II
by Barry Reid
Eden Press
PO Box 8410
Fountain Valley, CA 92728

HOW TO DISAPPEAR COMPLETELY
AND NEVER BE FOUND
by Doug Richmond
Loompanics Unlimited
PO Box 1197
Port Townsend, WA 98368

THE REAL WORLD OF
ALTERNATE I.D. ACQUISITION
by D.P. Rochelle
Paladin Press

HOW TO USE MAIL DROPS
FOR PRIVACY AND PROFIT
by Jack Luger
Loompanics Unlimited

DIRECTORY OF U.S. MAIL DROPS
compiled by Michael Hoy
Loompanics Unlimited

FRAUDULENT CREDENTIALS
U.S. House of Representatives Report
Loompanics Unlimited

HANDBOOK OF VITAL RECORDS
INFORMATION FOR ATTORNEYS
AND WELFARE WORKERS
Loompanics Unlimited

CREDIT: THE CUTTING EDGE
by Scott French
CEP, Inc.
PO Box 865
Boulder, CO 80306

CONSULAR ANTI-FRAUD HANDBOOK
U.S. Department of State
Paladin Press

PASSPORT AGENT'S MANUAL
U.S. Department of State
Loompanics Unlimited

BIRTH CERTIFICATE FRAUD
U.S. Inspector General
Loompanics Unlimited

SOCIAL SECURITY NUMBER FRAUD
Office of Inspector General
Eden Press

BEAR'S GUIDE TO EARNING
NON-TRADITIONAL COLLEGE DEGREES
by John Bear
Ten Speed Press
PO Box 7123
Berkeley, CA 94707

COMPARITIVE DATA:
STATE AND PROVINCIAL
LICENSING SYSTEMS
U.S. Department of Transportation
Loompanics Unlimited

DRIVER LICENSE
APPLICANT IDENTIFICATION
U.S. Department of Transportation
Loompanics Unlimited

VANISH!
by Johnny Yount
Paladin Press

HOW TO STEAL A JOB
by Bill Connors
Morrison Peterson Publishing
PO Box 25130
Honolulu, HI 96825

I.D. CHECKING GUIDE
Drivers License Guide Co.
PO Box 5305
Redwood City, CA 94063

DOCUMENT PREPARATION
by C.W.L
The Technology Group
PO Box 93124
Pasadena, CA 91109

I.D. BY MAIL
by Barry Reid
Eden Press

**HOW INTELLIGENCE AGENTS
CHANGE THEIR FINGERPRINTS**
by William Wilson
Alpha Publications
PO Box 92
Sharon Center, OH 44274

**REBORN IN THE U.S.A.,
Expanded Second Edition**
by Trent Sands
Loompanics Unlimited

- APPENDIX ONE -
MAJOR
CANADIAN
NEWSPAPERS

ALBERTA:
The Edmonton Journal, Edmonton
The Calgary Herald, Calgary

BRITISH COLUMBIA:
The Vancouver Sun, Vancouver
The Province, Vancouver
The Times-Colonist, Victoria

MANITOBA:
Winnipeg Free Press, Winnipeg

NEW BRUNSWICK:
St. John Times-Globe, St. John

NEWFOUNDLAND:
>*St. John's Telegram,* St. John's

NOVA SCOTIA:
>*Halifax Chronicle-Herald,* Halifax
>*Halifax Mail-Star,* Halifax

ONTARIO:
>*The Toronto Star,* Toronto
>*The Globe And Mail,* Toronto
>*The Ottawa Citizen,* Ottawa
>*The Windsor Star,* Windsor

QUEBEC:
>*La Presse,* Montreal
>*Montreal Gazette,* Montreal (English)
>*Le Soleil,* Quebec City

SASKATCHEWAN:
>*The Leader Post,* Regina
>*The Star-Phoenix,* Saskatoon

- APPENDIX TWO -
CANADIAN
TOURISM
DEPARTMENTS

ALBERTA:
Travel Alberta
15th Floor, 10025 Jasper Avenue
Edmonton, Alberta, T5J-323

BRITISH COLUMBIA:
Tourism British Columbia
Parliament Buildings
Victoria, British Columbia, V8V-1X4

MANITOBA:
Travel Manitoba
Dept. 9254, 7th Floor
155 Carlton Street
Winnipeg, Manitoba, R3C-3H8

NEW BRUNSWICK:
Tourism New Brunswick
PO Box 12345
Fredericton, New Brunswick, E3B-5C3

NEWFOUNDLAND:
Department of Tourism
PO Box 2016
St. John's, Newfoundland, A1C-5R8

NOVA SCOTIA:
Department of Tourism
PO Box 456
Halifax, Nova Scotia, B3J-2R5

ONTARIO:
Ministry of Tourism
Queens Park
Toronto, Ontario, M7A-2E5

QUEBEC:
Tourisme Quebec
CP 20000
Quebec City, Quebec, G1K-7X2

SASKATCHEWAN:
Tourism Saskatchewan
1919 Saskatchewan Drive
Regina, Saskatchewan, S4P-3V7

- APPENDIX THREE -
CANADIAN
DRIVERS LICENSE
OFFICES

ALBERTA:
> Motor Vehicles Div.
> 10001 Bellamy Hill
> Edmonton, Alberta, T5J-3B7
> (403) 427-7048

BRITISH COLUMBIA:
> Motor Vehicle Dept.
> Driver License Div.
> 2631 Douglas St.
> Victoria, British Columbia, V8T-5A3
> (604) 387-6824

MANITOBA:
Dept. of Highways & Transportation
1075 Portage Avenue
Winnipeg, Manitoba, R3G-0S1
(204) 945-6850

NEW BRUNSWICK:
Motor Vehicle Div.
PO Box 6000
Fredericton, New Brunswick, E3B-5H1
(506) 453-2810

NEWFOUNDLAND:
Motor Registration Div.
Viking Bldg.
Wishingwell Rd.
St. John's, Newfoundland
(709) 726-6110

NOVA SCOTIA:
Dept. of Transportation
Licenses & Registrations
PO Box 1652
Halifax, Nova Scotia, B3J-2Z3
(902) 424-5531

ONTARIO:
Ministry of Trans. & Comms.
East Bldg.
2680 Keele Street
Downsview, Ontario, M3M-3E6
(416) 244-1115

PRINCE EDWARD ISLAND:
Highway Safety Div.
PO Box 2000
Charlottetown, PEI, C1A-7N8
(902) 892-5306

QUEBEC:
Regie de l'Assurance
Automobile de Quebec
880, Ste-Foy Rd.
Quebec, Quebec, G1S-4N2
(418) 643-5523

SASKATCHEWAN:
Highway Traffic Board
2260 11th Ave
Regina, Saskatchewan, S4P-0J9
(306) 565-4020

NORTHWEST TERRITORIES:
Vehicle Registry
Dept. of Government Service
Yellowknife, NWT, X1A-2L9
(403) 873-7401

YUKON TERRITORY:
Registrar of Motor Vehicles
Box 2703
Whitehorse, YK, Y1A-2C6
(403) 667-5811

- APPENDIX FOUR -
EXCERPTS FROM THE
PRIVACY COMMISSIONER'S
1986 ANNUAL REPORT

Mandate

The *Privacy Act* provides individuals with access to their personal information held by the federal government; it protects individuals' privacy by limiting those who may see the information; and it gives the individual some control over the government's collection and use of the information.

The Act sets out the principles of fair information practices, requiring government to:

- collect only the information needed to operate its programs;

- collect the information directly from the individual concerned, whenever possible; and

- tell the individual how it will be used;
- keep the information long enough to ensure an individual access; and
- "take all reasonable steps" to ensure its accuracy and completeness.

Canadian citizens or permanent residents may complain to the Privacy Commissioner if:

- they are denied any part of the information;
- they are denied their request to correct some of the information on the file — or their right to annotate it;
- the department takes longer than the initial 30 days or maximum 60 days to provide the information;
- the Personal Information Index description of the contents of the information bank is deficient in some way;
- the department's listing in the Index does not describe all the uses it makes of personal information;
- an institution is collecting, keeping or disposing of personal information in a way which contravenes the *Privacy Act.*

Such complaints are investigated by the Privacy Commissioner by having his investigators examine any file (including those in closed banks) except confidences of the Queens Privy Council to ensure that government institutions are complying with the Act.

The Act also gives the Privacy Commissioner the power to audit the way government institutions are collecting, using and disposing of personal information, without having to wait for complaint.

Social Insurance Numbers

The Office of the Privacy Commissioner continues to receive many inquiries about social insurance numbers (SIN). For many persons a SIN is the focus and, unfortunately, the limit of privacy protection concerns. As such, it is important. The danger of singling out SINs for special treatment is that the protections of other personal information may seem less important and be neglected. SINs should be protected from indiscriminate and trivializing uses. But so should all personal information.

A social insurance number is personal information as defined in the *Privacy Act.* It receives the same protection, no more or no less, than does any other identifier or item of personal information. The issue is whether this number is so important, so special, that it requires controls over its use beyond that already offered.

At present, no legislation restricts the use of social insurance numbers. There are, however, 11 laws or regulations giving federal agencies the authority to request a social insurance number. These are:

Unemployment Insurance Act, 1971
   and Unemployment Insurance Regulations

Immigration Act, 1976

Income Tax Act

Canada Pension Plan Act

Old Age Security Act

Canada Elections Act

Canadian Wheat Board Act

Race Track Supervision Regulations

(Criminal Code)
Gasoline Excise Tax Refund Regulations
(Excise Tax Act)
Canada Student Loans Regulations
(Canada Student Loans Act)
Family Allowances Regulations
(Family Allowances Act, 1973)

If a number is requested for any other purpose, an individual is simply not obliged to meet the request. Of course, by not providing the number, he or she may be denied the goods and services which are desired.

The arguments for special status deserve respect. Unwanted information linkage through a SIN may still be easier than through any other single piece of personal information. However, with new computers, that may not be true much longer.

Uncontrolled and general use of the SIN establishes a de facto national identifier with all its ominous and de-humanizing implications. But after a thorough study of the issue, the former Privacy Commissioner, Inger Hansen, opposed placing any legal restrictions upon using social insurance numbers. She argued that such would be a band-aid solution, and a dangerous one, for it would convey a false sense of privacy security. She felt that private identifiers would take the place of the SINs, though persons might think that their privacy was effectively protected because the law controlled the uses of the SIN.

Ms. Hansen's recommendations went beyond the narrow issue of SIN usage. She proposed that anyone collecting personal information of any kind be forced by law to disclose its intended uses. Uses not disclosed in advance, not consented to or authorized by law would be illegal.

SINs are not collected to be exchanged with other federal agencies: that would contradict the *Privacy Act*. Nor are the SINs, which government institutions are authorized by statute to collect, available to institutions or individuals outside government. Therefore, possession of another person's SIN should no more unlock personal information from government than using another person's name.

Section 19 — other governments' information

Subsection 19(1) of the *Privacy Act* reads:.

"Subject to subsection (2), the head of a government institution shall refuse to disclose any personal information requested under subsection 12(1) that was obtained in confidence from

(a) the government of a foreign state or an institution thereof;

(b) an international organization of states or an institution thereof;

(c) the government of a province or an institution thereof; or

(d) a municipal or regional government established by or pursuant to an Act of legislature of a province or an institution of such a government."

The purpose of such exemptions is clear enough: the exchange of information is part of the life-blood of modern governments. Without some assurance that information being given out will be protected by the receiving government, the most useful sources of supply could dry up. Governments also want to control their own information. They do not want sensitive data, held secure in their jurisdiction, to be released under the access laws of another jurisdiction. It is a matter of informational sovereignty and, in principle, that is entirely defensible.

What is not defensible are the blanket claims of confidentiality which have been declared by some provinces for all information they pass on to the federal government. In a federal state a vast amount of personal information is exchanged, one level of government to another. When a province unilaterally imposes confidentiality upon all information it shares with the federal government, significant amounts of personal information are automatically exempt from access. As the *Privacy Act* is now written, the federal government institution receiving personal information from a province, which has insisted upon a blanket of confidentiality, has no discretionary power. The instruction of section 19 is absolute: "The head of a government institution *shall* refuse to disclose."

The point has been made in the first two annual reports of the Privacy Commissioner; the *Privacy Act* may now be used to prevent an individual from receiving personal information which he or she might have received before the legislation was in effect. It is, of course, profoundly damaging to the credibility of the *Privacy Act* if confidentiality claims are not made for good and sufficient reasons.

On two occasions, the Privacy Commissioner made the following recommendations:

"The matter should not wait to be addressed until the parlimentary review. The Minister of Justice should draw the problem to the attention of his provincial colleagues, requesting their cooperation in protecting the integrity of the federal legislation. Without that cooperation, we face the paradox of an expanded *Privacy Act* reducing individuals' rights."

The Minister of Justice may indeed have raised this issue with the provincial attorneys' general. Unfortunately, section 19 and confidentiality blankets still prevent a significant number of individuals from receiving personal information to which they would be otherwise entitled.

Investigators from the Privacy Commissioner's Office have been instructed to ask federal custodians of provincially-originated information to seek release of personal information by provincial authorities on a case-by-case basis. This approach was taken when provincial authorities, in response to the Privacy Commissioner's complaint, said that they wanted the opportunity to review each request and that they would be disposed to authorize releases in the spirit of the *Privacy Act*.

Unfortunately, the formal claim of confidentiality is usually given more respect than statements of goodwill. Most federal institutions play it safe — and easy. They remain reluctant to get behind the general prohibition and unresolved complaints pile up in the Privacy Commissioner's Office.

Section 19 remains a major source of frustration to applicants for personal information and to the administration of the *Privacy Act*.

There are two possible solutions:

1) remove the absolute protection which the *Privacy Act* now gives all information coming from sources outside the federal government;

2) convince provinces to withdraw claims of total confidentiality.

When provinces adopt privacy legislation of their own, individuals will be able to apply directly for personal information under provincial control. As this happens, section 19 should become a less significant problem. In addition, provinces committed to the fair information practices represented by privacy laws are not as likely to make excessive confidentiality demands. But these hopes are of no help at all to those whose personal information is now captive of section 19.

Role of the Privacy Commissioner

Exempt Information Banks

One of the most sensitive and vexed issues arising during the first years of the *Privacy Act* is the status of and necessity for what are called, in the jargon of the privacy trade, exempt banks. Some history is indispensable.

Little concern was expressed about exempt banks during the legislative passage of the *Privacy Act*. It seemed straightforward enough: section 18 gave the Governor-in-Council the right to "designate as exempt banks certain personal information banks" containing files all of which consisted "predominately" of personal information of a particularly sensitive nature. Information qualifying a bank as exempt would be that which, for example, "could reasonably be expected to be injurious to the conduct of international affairs, the defense of Canada" or personal information obtained or prepared in the course of criminal investigations.

When the Act came into effect, 19 (of some 2,200) banks were designated as closed; following a complaint to the Privacy Commissioner, an additional bank was closed. Individuals who applied for personal information which might be contained in the closed banks were denied access, being given neither denial nor confirmation of the existence of information about them.

The Privacy Commissioner has the responsibility for the oversight of these closed banks. He may examine all personal records (except confidences of the Queen's Privy Council) in any bank in which personal information is kept. The Commissioner may recommend that files be removed from a bank, or material be removed from files and transferred to other banks, or that files be destroyed. He can do this while neither confirming nor denying the existence of a particular file, if that has been the position of the department. He does, however, assure a complainant that he, an independent officer, has looked at the files in these banks and that the complainant's privacy rights have been respected.

The status of these exempt banks was challenged following the application of Nick Ternette for personal information from RCMP bank P-130, Security Service Records (now SIS-P-PU-010). The RCMP would neither confirm nor deny the existence of the bank of any personal information about the applicant. Mr. Ternette complained to the Privacy Commissioner who investigated and found that he too could neither confirm nor deny the existence of any record. He told Mr. Ternette his rights had been respected and advised him of his right to appeal to the Federal Court of Canada for a review of the RCMP's refusal of his application.

Mr. Ternette appealed. His lawyers asked the Department of Justice to confirm that all the files in the bank had been examined before it was closed to determine if the bank met the criteria for exemption. The Department of Justice responded that the files had not been individually reviewed and that the bank should now be treated as an open bank.

Such new treatment does not mean that the power to exempt sensitive files have been diminished in any essential way. Personal information in this or any bank may not be released if exemptions provided in the *Privacy Act* can be applied. But losing exempt status does mean that a file can be exempt, only after a specific, new examination, and not merely because it is found in a special bank.

The Department of Justice's inability to defend the validity of the RCMP's exempt bank forced the Privacy Commissioner to abandon an original working assumption that exempt banks were properly closed.

The Privacy Commissioner has a special responsibility, because of the uniqueness of his access, to examine closed banks for compliance with the *Privacy Act.* When the office first opened for business, he had to assume the validity of the exemption of each of the 19 banks from the general right of access. Without making such an assumption, it would have been impossible to carry out the immediate and pressing duty of investigating all complaints. In fact, had the original investigation staff of four persons been set to work on examining closed banks, complaint-answering would have been indefinitely delayed, effectively denying many applicants their privacy rights.

In January 1985 the compliance branch of the Privacy Commissioner's Office began a systematic examination of all closed banks. The first to be investigated were two banks of Employment and Immigration Canada, EIC/P-PU-260 (Immigration Security and Intelligence Data Bank) and EIC/P-PU-265 (Enforcement Information Index System). These banks were chosen for the administrative convenience of the Privacy Commissioner's Office, not because of any special concern. The Commissioner was unable to examine the documents which established the basis upon which the Governor-in-Council closed the banks because these documents are confidences of the Queen's Privy Council. However, the investigation found evidence that individual files had not been examined prior to the application for exempt status.

The Privacy Commissioner informed the deputy minister that since the banks did not meet the criteria of the *Privacy Act*, he would treat any complaints relating to these banks in the same manner as those against open banks.

The Privacy Commissioner also asked deputy ministers responsible for all other closed banks to advise him whether files in these banks were properly examined before a submission for exemption was made to the Governor-in Council. On the basis of the replies and planned systematic audits, findings will be made as to compliance of the exempt banks with the provisions of the *Privacy Act*.

Any banks which, in the opinion of the Privacy Commissioner, were improperly constituted will be treated as open. Though this involves a fundamental change in the handling of the personal information in such banks, the change is not sweeping so far as the ability to exempt information is concerned.

Yet there is some gain from the data protection standpoint. Each application will require the institution to examine the file, not to reject the request automatically because of the privileged position of an information bank. Government institutions may regret the loss of an easy denial of access. But applicants for personal information will be assured of receiving individual treatment.

From the Privacy Commissioner's point of view, there is another advantage in the loss of exempt status. The very fact that whole banks of personal information are excluded from access discourages persons from using the *Privacy Act* and fosters skepticism about the usefulness of the legislation. Opening up these closed banks should enhance the credibility of the *Privacy Act.*

In summary: The concept of exempt banks remains defensible. Their disadvantages perhaps make them dispensible.

The Privacy Act and You

What information does the government have about me?

Without knowing your personal circumstances we can't tell exactly what information the federal government has about you. No single file in Ottawa contains everything about you; there are a number of files depending on what contacts you have had with the government.

Some information on most Canadian residents will turn up as a result of at least one of the following:

Income tax files
UIC contributions
CPP deductions or benefits
Student loan applications
Social insurance number applications
Passport applications
Old age security benefits
Customs declarations

Perhaps your name appears in the files of those who have applied for a home insulation grant or who have auditioned at the National Arts Centre.

If you have ever worked for the federal government, your department and the Public Service Commission may still have your personnel file, a record of any job competitions you entered, your annual performance appraisal, any applications for parking spaces and information about your pay and benefits. The Personal Information Index will indicate how long these files are kept.

Where do I find The Personal Information Index?

Copies of the Index are available at public and federal departmental libraries, and some rural post offices, along with the forms needed to apply for access. The Personal Information Index explains what each institution does, how to apply for access, and lists the files each government institution keeps.

One section lists files concerning the public; another, federal employees. If you believe there is information about you but cannot find an appropriate bank listed in the Index, the Act still ensures you access if you can provide the department with sufficient specific information for it to be found by staff.

How do I see personal information about me?

From the Index, determine which banks could contain information about you. Complete a Personal Information Request Form for each bank you wish to examine and send it to the coordinator listed under each institution. There is no charge. The department must respond within 30 days of receiving your request but may ask for a 30-day extension.

Are there information banks I can't see?

Yes. However, following a court challenge to one of the closed banks the status of the original 20 is in question. Many are now being treated as open, although much of the material may still be exempt under other provisions of the *Privacy Act.*

Individuals who are interested in personal files which may be in an exempt bank should apply to the department in question and await its response.

The following departments still consider these banks closed:

Privy Council Office	PCO/P-PU-005, Security and Intelligence Information Files
Canadian Security Intelligence Service	SIS/P-PU-010, Canadian Security Intelligence Service Records
National Defense	DND/P-PU-040 CSE, Security and Intelligence Investigation Files
RCMP	CMP/P-PU-055, Protection of Personnel and Government Property
Solicitor General	SGC/P-PU-025, Security Policy and Operations Records SGC/P-PU-055, Commissions of Inquiry SGC/P-PU-030, Police and Law Enforcement Records Relating to the Security and Safety of Persons and Property in Canada SGC/P-PU-035, Protection of Privacy (wiretapping —Criminal Code)

Does this mean I may see everything else?

No, not quite. Some material in other banks may be excluded because the personal information:

— was received in confidence from a municipal, provincial or national government;

— could injure Canada's defense or conduct of its affairs;

— was collected by an investigative body during the investigation of a crime;

— could threaten an individual's safety;

— is the subject of a solicitor-client privilege;

— relates to an individual's mental or physical health if the knowledge could be contrary to his/her best interest (the information may be released to the person's doctor);

— concerns security clearances (although this exemption is not mandatory);

— is a confidence of the Queen's Privy Council;

— was obtained by Correctional Service Canada or the National Parole Board while the person making the request was under sentence for an offense against any act of Parliament, if the disclosure "could reasonably be expected to"

• lead to a serious disruption of the person's institutional, parole or mandatory supervision program, or

• reveal information about the person obtained originally on a promise of confidentiality, either express or implied.

Can the government disclose my personal information to someone else?

The act generally requires a government institution to obtain your permission before it releases personal information. However, there are several circumstances when your consent is not required. Personal information may be released:

— to comply with another act of Parliament;

— to comply with a warrant or subpoena;

— for the Attorney General of Canada to use in a legal proceeding;

— for the use of an investigative body (such as the RCMP or Military Police) when enforcing a law;

— to another government in order to administer or enforce a law when there is an arrangement between the two governments;

— to a member of Parliament who is trying to help you (with your consent);

— to carry out an official audit;

— to the Public Archives for storage;

— for statistical or research purposes providing that the researcher agrees in writing not to disclose the information;

— to help native people prepare claims;

— to collect a debt to the Crown or to pay an individual a debt owed by the Crown;

— to further the public interest;

— or to benefit you. (In these last two cases the institution must notify the Privacy Commissioner who may in turn notify you.)

Which government departments are covered by the Privacy Act?

Most of the federal departments, agencies and commissions are covered by the Act but not those Crown corporations which compete with the private sector as do CBC, Air Canada and CN.

What can I do if I think the information is incorrect?

Write to the privacy coordinator at the institution holding the information, explaining the error and setting out the corrections you would like made. Generally there is little difficulty correcting factual errors. If you are refused, you have the right to attach a notation to the information showing the correction you wanted made.

What should I do if I have been refused access?

If it is not clear to you why the institution has refused your request, the first step is to ask the appropriate privacy coordinator to explain the problem to you. Many departments and agencies will accept collect calls. Perhaps there has been a misunderstanding.

If, after talking to the coordinator, you still think you have been wrongly denied the information, call or write to the Privacy Commissioner's office.

The Privacy Commissioner of Canada
112 Kent Street, 14th Floor
Ottawa, Ontario
Canada K1A 1H3
(613) 995-2410
1-800-267-0441 (The switchboard is open from 7:30 a.m. to 6:00 p.m., Ottawa time.)

YOU WILL ALSO WANT TO READ: